PITCHSLAPPED

THE ART OF SERVING, NOT SELLING

Juliet Dillon Clark

First Edition

Ghostwriting by Kristy Boyd Johnson

ISBN 9781513662336

CONTENTS

ACKNOWLEDGEMENTS

A good book is always a group effort. While the ideas expressed here are mine, there are many people who put hard work into encouraging me and helping to make this book possible.

I would like to thank my writing coach and friend Kristy Boyd Johnson for her help and support getting the ideas on paper in an organized fashion. She has been indispensable over the years in the growth of my writing skills. My hope is that every writing journey has someone like Kristy along for the ride.

Another big thanks to Tracy Hazzard for her support and for adding credibility to my ideas by writing the Foreword.

Last but not least....thanks to my children, Ally and Ty, for always bringing me back down to earth by declaring that they have never read any of my books and probably never will. I love you two to the moon and back.

INTRODUCTION

THE VICIOUS CYCLE EXPERTS FACE

I f you are like most authors, coaches, and speakers you are passionate about what you do and want to leave a legacy in the world. Many of you have a dream of writing a book and creating courses that will help others improve their quality of life. We also want to make money and scale our businesses so we have more free time.

Yes, it's a lovely story... until the realities of the coaching world hit. If you write a book, it's not so easy as "post your book on Amazon and they will come." If you have programs and services, it's not so easy to post on social media and hope they come. Let's be honest, the "if you build it, they will come" mentality from "Field of Dreams" only works for Kevin Costner. Even then, it only worked because he has name recognition, a movie studio, lots of money behind the PR machine and oh....it was fiction.

The coaching industry is the only industry I can think of where you go to a business seminar and when you leave, someone tries to sell you on a coaching program. You are presented with about $200,000 worth of coaches and you don't have a viable, sustainable product. It's crazy! If you don't have that kind of money to spend without the promise of income, you are left running around trying to gain attention from people who have no idea who you are. And, if you are sending out blind emails, well, that amounts to nothing more than spam.

Big no-no.

It is also the only industry where I can declare myself an expert on a topic with no real training to support my expertise. This may be one of the main reasons that "experts" are conned into spending all of the money on training without having an actual area of expertise. I talk to people every week who have decided that they are experts in areas that only licensed professionals should be experts in. Case in point: a person who helps teens avoid suicide. This is a great mission, no doubt. Being a Reiki master or a life coach is not a qualification for this type of work. This is delicate work that needs to be handled by a trained, licensed professional. Some of the so-called experts out there can do more harm than good. Yet, I talk to people every week that have missions like this.

Here's the problem: *most authors, coaches, and speakers are so busy creating that they make the big mistake of thinking either 1) My product is so awesome that everyone needs it, or 2) I don't need to test my ideas and connect with my target consumers before the project is complete.*

That means these unfortunate entrepreneurs are always playing catch-up, because they start out way behind the curve. And, because they are playing catch-up instead of getting out in front of the curve, they find themselves in such a discouraging place of getting nowhere that most just give up.

So how do you change this vicious cycle into a sustainable business? One that works for you and your ideal clients?

Here's the key: *all entrepreneurs should start testing the market and having conversations with their ideal clients while they are creating.* That means knowing your target audience, talking to your target audience, building a platform, and being ready by the time your program, book, or service is actually on the market.

Right now, you're probably saying, "Well, I want to be seen, and I want a bestseller, but I just want to create first and have people flock to me. I don't want to have to do any marketing or have conversations until I am done."

No. This is the brutal truth of the vicious cycle: regardless of who you *think* your target market is, you must validate. Until you have validated, you are in danger of wasting time and money on a product that will not sell. Until you have had conversations and tested, it is all a big guess. What small business has cash to burn guessing who their ideal client is?

The unfortunate fact is this: most authors, coaches, and speakers are unprepared for what this coaching/ speaking/ publishing process really is. The great self-promoters in the industry want you to think it is an easy, instant gratification business. The truth is that it is not.

In this book, you'll learn what you need to know to get way ahead of the curve, identify your ideal audience, build a platform to serve that audience, and prepare yourself for the new life you seek to build.

ABOUT THE AUTHOR
MY PERSONAL JOURNEY

always wanted to write a book and just never really had the time. Then 2007 found me in the midst of an ugly divorce. Isn't that how most good things start? In the middle of ugliness. All of a sudden, I only had kids half of the week. Writing became a time-filler for me as well as a way to heal.

My divorce was horrible. Nasty and ugly. No one could behave like adults. My first novel sprung from frustration and the fact that I had the sick, twisted, and totally normal desire to kill my ex-husband. That is how my first book *Players* began...with a murder. Not just any murder...if you look at a picture of my ex-husband and the description of the first victim, you will get that I got my wish and "murdered" my husband. It was cathartic and fun all at the same time. The best part? No risk of jail. Let's face it, felony orange is not a good color for blondes. Thank God felons don't wear royal blue, or this story could have ended in a real- life drama.

When it came time to publish, I decided to use a self-publisher. Here's where it gets interesting. Right out of college, I worked for a traditional publisher. I had a lot of insight into what the publishing world was and wasn't. After I signed a contract with a large, well-known self-publisher, a couple of things became apparent. First, some unethical self-publishers sell writers many services that they do not need and that do not benefit them.

Case in point: I could have spent an enormous amount of money to have my book release sent out to the publisher's email list of over a million people. Sounds good, right? But, since these were not people who were part of my target market, but rather people who wanted to publish books, it was not an effective marketing tool for me. In other words, I was paying the publisher to promote themselves (not me).

The second realization came when it was time to calculate royalties. My book was overpriced because the publisher was marking up the actual cost of the book. So, if a book costs $2.50 to print, the publisher was marking it up 100% and charging the consumer $9.95, but also keeping a big piece of those back-end profits. Now, if this were a traditional publisher, of course this would be an okay practice because they don't charge any upfront fees to publish your book. Consider this: you paid a self-publisher to produce your book, and then they charge you more to actually print your book and keep a big percentage of the royalties. That business model was not in the author's favor…at all.

My first book flopped, which was all right with me because I learned some valuable lessons along the way. By the time I completed book two, I had my own self-publishing company. Instead of making $1.59 a copy, I was making $5.62 a copy. My second book was where my platform-building skills came into play. I created a following on Facebook, Twitter, and Google Plus. At the same time, I was building a business presence as well. When my second book published, sales were better because I had built a following. The lessons that kicked in were more about my self-publishing company exposure than my book.

Having worked on two billion-dollar marketing accounts after leaving publishing, I knew quite a bit about marketing. Working on the Nissan Regional account at Chiat/ Day Advertising gave me a glimpse at what regional ad campaigns looked like and how they were uniquely targeted at a different avatars because markets varied in different areas of the country. After being on Google Plus for a while, I realized that the people who were following me there were a bunch of starving artists. They were nice people, yes, but would never buy anything. Lesson learned. I began to focus more on Facebook and LinkedIn.

By my third book, I had sold over 25,000 copies of some relatively bad mystery novels. The good news was that more and more people were coming to my company to publish. The bad news was that they were coming out of business seminars where they were being told that they needed a book to be considered an expert. That was a great pitch, but reality was that most of these people had products and services that weren't selling, and they thought that a book was the magic bullet.

Let me be clear.... there is no magic bullet in platform building. It is all strategic marketing.

For many of these potential entrepreneurial experts, I foresaw another failed product in a book. Even worse, many of these people learned how to build beginning funnels. The problem was that none of them knew about conversion and how to drive traffic. All of this added up to one big marketing disaster and many good books never being read.

What was missing? A platform. Many of these people never built marketing for their product, services, or their books. That's when we began teaching potential authors how to build a platform. There is a sequence to platform building that is crucial.

This all begins with foundational tools. Who is your ideal audience? This is not a guess. Businesses do not seek capital from investors without market research. Most of these new authors built coaching businesses without marketing research. Many of them never connected with their ideal client before developing products and services and were guessing at what the needs of these clients were. In short, no one knew who they were and what they did, not because they needed an expert book, but because they were in front of the wrong audiences with the wrong products.

At the same time, I was working on my new business, I began going out to networking groups frequently and marketing online. The one thing that stood out for me in both instances was how soon people pitched their businesses. It felt sleazy and uncomfortable. Yes, I love to tell people about my business, but this felt like desperation. Why were these people pitching me? In most cases, I wouldn't have thought of myself as their ideal client. I was invited to "coffee" almost every week. The first couple times I went, I found out that "coffee" was code for let me pitch you! There were times during coffee that I wished I drank and we could make this cocktails. At least then, the pitch would have been palatable.

I can't tell you how many groups I attended, only to find out that the members weren't quality players. They turned out to be people who gathered for breakfast or lunch once a week and asked for referrals. I was part of a group for a brief time where everyone smiled at one of the business owners and behind his back recommended that women not work with him. "He doesn't work well with women." When I became president of these lovely people, I tried to change the status quo and bring some education and training to the group. That was a big "NO." No one wanted to grow and learn, they just wanted to have breakfast, pitch, and get referrals. It was maddening!

You will find, in this book, that foundational tools include building avatars, using assessment marketing to connect with an audience, and discover what they want and need. This is not a system of surveying. Assessment marketing is a system that allows you to find out more about your ideal consumer, and a lead-generation system so you know exactly who to talk to and who to let go of.

My hope is, that by the time you complete this book, you will have a better understanding of how to build an assessment platform and know more about your ideal consumer that will help you sell more books, products, and services in a sustainable way.

CHAPTER 1

PITCHSLAPPED

H ave you ever been to a networking group or event where the person in front of you goes from hello directly into a pitch to sell you something? You have no idea who they are or what kind of reputation they have and there they are throwing a pitch at you. You stand there, smiling and nodding, but not listening at all. I'll bet you walked away feeling like someone just dumped a bucket of mud over your head – dirty, embarrassed, and a little shell-shocked.

This is how most people try to get business. As a society, we have become instant-gratification lovers and forgotten the art of building a relationship. In order to better serve your ideal client, you need to know them and build trust through service.

Back in my real estate days, a couple called me in distress. They were upside down on their condo and needed comps to determine their next move. I knew that they were in no position to sell because they were so underwater with their loans. I ran comps for them and sat and explained what was going on with the other condos in their complex. They were able to use the information to negotiate a loan modification on their second loan. They called me periodically while they were in the process of modifying the loan to ask questions. I kept in touch with this couple for many years after, mostly calling to see how they were doing and if things had eased up for them. Seven years later, they called me to tell me that one of them had inherited some money and asked if I could help them sell their condo and move to a ranch. People remember great service with no strings attached. They also remember that you cared enough to keep in touch and find out what they are up to.

One of the most untapped areas of sales is conversations with past clients and your circle of influence. It is important to keep your contacts up to date and reach out every couple of months to all of these people to keep you and your services top of mind. Debbie Hoffman the CEO and founder of Power Up Your Follow Up, works with small businesses on their sales follow up. What is most surprising to her is that they don't have a Customer Relationship Management (CRM) system. You need this type of system to keep track of contacts, buying patterns, and conversations.

From my days in real estate and working with the Mike Ferry and Tom Ferry organizations, reaching out to your sphere of influence and past clients was one of the ways successful real estate agents kept themselves top of mind. I had these tasks scheduled every three months in my calendar. Most of the time, I didn't have to ask for a referral. Through the real estate transaction, you build a relationship, so most of my calls were just to catch up on the lives of the people in my life. Again, referrals came because as a business owner I demonstrated that I cared.

Service Strategy

There is little else that will make your business successful other than good marketing and sales. That is why good businesses can become popular and great businesses sometimes fail. That is why movements sell products. The service- conversion model represents the way to move interest from engagement to conversion. The good news is that you will be able to use this model for your business once you understand what is driving most marketers and how you can set yourself apart. All of this falls into place.

The challenge of marketing in today's crowded environment has become an epidemic of "Look-at-Me" marketing. The Internet and airways are cluttered with a sea of marketing messages, calls-to-action, and invitations that are all born out of what we call "Look-at-Me" messages, which are free offers that invite you to learn about their expertise, experience, and their brilliance and discover how you can help with the challenge they face. While this is often effective marketing strategy for showcasing your abilities to impact powerful change, it can also communicate a message that is more egocentric and miss the most important element... the client!

The solution is the addition of "Look-at-You" calls-to-action. Imagine if in addition to the client discovering what you have to offer, they could also receive a gift of clarity about what's not working for them and where they need to create some shifts to experience the results they desire. With this "Look-at-You" approach to lead generation and relationship building, we shine the light on the potential clients, rather than on you. This allows them to get their head out of the sales pitch and shine the light on where they are in the process and what they truly need. Here in lies the magic of "service-driven" lead generation.

Service-Driven Lead Generation is about relationships, not clicks. It is about putting yourself out there. Entrepreneurs have become so used to the "click mentality" that they don't engage in good old-fashion networking. Face-to-face connection where you hear the story of the person you are connecting with. Service-driven marketing works because we care more about what is happening for our clients and potential clients than we do about self-promotion. Look around on Facebook today, what do you see? You see ads that communicate instant gratification success like anything that is "6 Figures in 6 Months." You also see ads for lifestyle; look at my beautiful house, my beautiful car, my beautiful wife/husband. (I hope I didn't just plagiarize a Talking Heads song). Most of these "look at me" ads are run by people who are great self-promoters, not great deliverers. People want to work with experts who get results.

This instant gratification messaging doesn't just apply to Facebook ads. I recently saw a group where the business owner shared his own story about making "40k in Six Days" and now he is going to share the script that created this magic! I asked for a copy of the "magic" script (he was giving it to everyone that asked). It was a fluff piece of self-promotion. Push and salesy and a big turn off. He suggested that you use Facebook Messenger to spread this message. I was appalled. Why? Ask anyone who gets these types of messages in Facebook Messenger or LinkedIn. Most will tell you they HATE them and have sworn to never do business with people who do this.

A second story about Facebook groups that promise these types of results. A group owner recently created a program for "his people" where they could make "100k in 90 days by Creating a Facebook Group." I showed interest and asked for a money-back guarantee. Crickets....and I was no longer in the group. Whoa....I was ex-communicated for asking if he stood behind his results? His actions indicated that it was a big, fat NO!

Here are a few reasons why a Service-Driven Lead Generation strategy works:

1. Is aligned with your desire to serve and contribute on a bigger scale.

2. Helps clients discover "what's off" in areas where you can help them grow.

3. Is a fresh approach that allows you to stand out among your competition.

4. Uses unique qualities of "intrigue" and "inquiry" to capture the potential client's attention and create curiosity.

The key tool that drives service-driven lead generation is the use of a short assessment. This should be a short (no longer than 20 questions) assessment that takes only three to five minutes for the potential clients to take. All questions should be worded in a way that allows the answer to be on a sliding 1-10 scale. Feedback should come back to you to assess if there is potential for more commitment to other programs, products, or services. A copy also goes back to the person who took the assessment, so an accurate picture of their skill level is in their hands.

So how do you create service relationships? Be intentional about who you are attracting. The challenge that most business owners face with so many options for marketing is how to choose and which to implement. In my own business and coaching, I have found a myriad of marketing possibilities in three categories. While not every strategy is represented in the three suggestions below, this does represent the most popular and cost-effective marketing strategies used by experts and thought leaders to attract and engage new clients. We will be referencing many of these strategies as you incorporate your assessment into your marketing efforts from this point forward.

Attraction begins with having connections and a support/ referral system. Collaboration is an amazing way to build relationships that will help you build your list and network. However, you need to have all of the pieces of your funnel in place before partners will be willing to work with you. This usually requires:

1. Free gift (the assessment
2. Opt-in with affiliate link
3. A back-end campaign (webinar/ weekly show, promotional email swipes, social media promotional pieces)

The assessment as an opt-in is a new shift in the lead magnet paradigm. For years, we have used a lead magnet as the goody to entice someone to give us an email address. The truth? It worked for a while. People were excited about it until they realized the transference of your genius gave you the right to SPAM them to death.

In 2017, my company surveyed people who had opted into a lead magnet at some time on the last year. 62% of those people told us that they opted in and never opened the content that was sent to them. About 30% told us that they used the lead magnet and never had any intention of hiring the person they received it from. They were Do-It-Yourselfers who just wanted "the free stuff." In other words, the exchange of the guru's genius for an email address wasn't working.

You probably noticed a shift around that time to a $7 lead magnet. The test was whether these people would pull out a credit card because free had no value. That idea didn't work well either. The bottom line: people were exhausted by all of the offers that had nothing to really do with them. No one was asking the consumer what they really wanted.

The assessment as an opt-in for a campaign or affiliate gives the consumer an opportunity to assess where their skillset is in relationship to success. They are measuring where they are in the process of their goals, and the business owners are getting some great information to make their businesses better. It is a win/win.

The assessment is also a great way to accumulate statistical information. If you want to JV partner with anyone, know this: the larger the promotional players is in the industry, the more they are going to scrutinize your campaign before saying yes. This means that you must have statistical information for them that shows them that their audience is the right audience for your product. Collaboration partners are usually looking for what is in it for them. That means that they are looking for product commission that makes sense for their effort and their list. Think 40 to 50%.

Content is Critical to Building Trust

Content is the tool that establishes your expertise. You are showing people that you know what you are talking about without self-promoting. You will generate much more interest in your expertise if people can hear you speak or read an article you have generated. This is also the tool, in conjunction to your Call-to-Action (CTA), to transition people out of events and social media and into your email list.

Let me tell you a story about what this looks like when you don't transition from social media to your list.

One of my friends had an amazing online magazine on MySpace. With over 300,000 hits a month, she was making her living from developing content good enough to attract sponsorships. Then Facebook hit the scene and people left MySpace in droves. Because she never transitioned any of those people into her email list, she lost her sponsors and lost her income.

Can you imagine the power of having all of those people on her list and sending out a couple emails telling everyone that the magazine moved to a new location on Facebook? She could have become a first-generation influencer on the biggest platform on the web. Look at this as a cautionary tale; it could happen to you tomorrow.

Before you transition people from social media to your list, relationship-building is established by conscious content and posting that provides value. Every planned piece of content invites the consumer to take a bigger step towards commitment because you are establishing yourself as the go-to person for your product.

Using assessments and service-driven engagement strategy provides different points in your marketing funnel to re-engage and re-market to your list.

Service-driven tactics also serve your potential clients once they are inside of your list. You can use assessments to create opportunities to offer strategy sessions and sales-closing conversations. Inside of your list, you also have an opportunity to create smaller assessments to find out what people want more of. This sort of "digital listening" will keep your audience engaged. These are strategies you would have little success increasing in numbers if you spammed on social media without building a relationship.

Find out more about using content to build your platform in our Promote, Profit, Publish interview with Podetize owner, Tracy Hazzard: https://superbrandpublishing.com/how-to-grow-you r-platform-with-tracy-hazzard/

CHAPTER 2

WHAT DO YOUR CLIENTS WANT? SHUT UP AND LISTEN!

This seems so easy, right? Yet, this is the main reason most books, products, and services fail: we don't shut up and listen! We jump in and make assumptions about who we serve, without a profile about our consumer. For those who do create a profile, many times, they proceed to product creation without validating that our assumptions are correct.

Finding your target market can be a challenging task. Many in the coaching world write books to establish themselves as experts. Unfortunately, many of them are looking for clients in all of the wrong places. Not only are they not building the profiles they need to be successful, they are not connecting with the right people because they don't know where to find these people. The number one complaint that I hear consistently on enrollment calls is that they don't know where to find the people who can afford them. The assumption is that they will connect with these ideal people online. That online connection requires specific information that most new businesses don't think about. The Internet is a crazy place and you can't assume anything about the people you meet there. Try online dating and you will know exactly what I mean.

In short, many businesses go about the task of building their ideal client backwards. They create a product that they think there is a need for and then they seek their ideal client for the product. Before jumping into any project, it is important to build the avatar for your offerings. Whether it is a book, product, or service, your ideal consumer profile must be built, in detail, before it can be validated, and a product created. This includes demographics and psychographics (we will discuss this fully in Chapter 4). Why is this important? The better you know your consumer, the more you will be able to fully serve them.

In order to ascertain what your ideal client wants, you need to build a relationship with them and ask. Now, this doesn't mean that you go ask your family. Everyone knows that your mother thinks you are the best thing since sliced bread and will like everything you produce. You need to seek out people who have the problem you solve and ask and then be silent when they answer. When I say "ask," I don't mean post a question on social media - actually talk to them. There is a big disconnect that social media has created: we don't talk to people anymore. Have a conversation with someone about what they want and need. Not just one conversation, a hundred conversations. While you are at it, have conversations with people you don't know. Your friends may tell you what you want to hear. Strangers won't be so compassionate about your feelings and may tell you the truth.

Some people won't believe me on this, but I have personal experience. When I wrote my first book, my own best friend wouldn't read it. I bugged her incessantly about it. Finally, she told me, "If I read it and it sucks, I don't want to be the one who has to tell you." Yikes! She was probably more honest than most. Most of your friends will tell you that you and your product are awesome even if it isn't true.

Back in my advertising days, we would create focus groups with real people and ask questions. Focus groups were gatherings of ideal prospects/clients that we would ask questions about the product and get feedback. We conducted these groups at malls. Remember the person who used to approach you and ask you to come into a back room to view an ad or a movie clip? Unfortunately, if you did this in a mall today, someone would call security, but that doesn't mean you can't run a focus group of your own. This is what our consumers want...the ability to talk to us, connect, and feel heard. We have lost the art of relationship building and have exhausted prospects with digital programming. Running an online focus group on Zoom or having a Meet-Up group may be more modern ways to conduct this type of research.

Here are three areas to consider before you spend the time and money creating a product:

- What do my ideal clients really want?
- How do they want it delivered?
- How do I need to shift my models for my programs to deliver the right model?

Back in 2016, I sold a program from stage. It was a low-cost program ($997) and one that purchasers could work on at their own pace. When we invited purchasers to a call three months later to get feedback on the program, we discovered several useful pieces of information.

1. Many users had not finished. Some said they didn't have the time and motivation to complete on their own. Others

indicated that they got stuck and didn't know how to implement the strategy and never reached out for help. When we queried this further, many of these people told us that they don't buy programs like this anymore because they had a history of not finishing.

2. Almost 70% of the purchasers told us that they would be willing to pay more to be part of a group or one-on-one program to get the support and motivation to get through the program and stay in action.

3. People wanted us to help build with them side-by-side, so they understood what they were doing.

These were amazing pieces of feedback for us. We took a $997 DIY product and transformed it into a $3,997 group product with some one-on-one support to get it up and running effectively. The result was that we just had an audience tell us that they would be willing to pay more for a different program structure. Not only did people buy the upgraded format, they started referring others. We went from about a 50% referral rate in 2017, to a 90% referral rate in 2019. The new model was working for people because now they had support and were getting the kind of results they wanted.

Exercise:

1. Take a deep-dive look at your existing programs and services. What is working? What is not working?

2. Do you have past clients who have taken these programs, or used these services, who can give you feedback about what they liked, what could have been done better, and

how you could improve the experience to achieve better results?

3. How soon can you gather this group of people who paid money for your program together for an online focus group?

CHAPTER 3

HOW TO FIND YOUR IDEAL MARKET

Now that you have taken a look at your programs and services, it is time to create some shifts in how you assess and build your target market more effectively. It is time to change the way you are talking to your market.

First of all, let go of the preconceived notions that you will identify the audience and they will come running. The number one waste of money out on the marketplace is the repeated hiring of marketing companies that turn around and ask you who and where your target market is. We hire a marketing company, they come up with a strategy to sell your products and services to an audience that you related was your audience. No marketing research of any kind other than key words. You don't actually know if you are in front of the right audience until your marketing succeeds, or in most cases fails.

The cure for this is to test your audience before you run a campaign and ads. You begin to ramp up spending when you know you are in front of the right audience. How will you know this? They will tell you. They will identify as a high commitment person who wants to solve the problem you solve and will be willing to spend money to do it. That is one of the beautiful things about assessment marketing; people tell you what they want and need.

Location, location, location...everyone related to real estate knows this phrase. For most entrepreneurs, their mantra should be validation, validation, validation. What does that mean? It means that you have a feedback loop that works to validate your audience, validate your product, and validate the purchase power of that product. This process is a hard look at what the success looks like if someone is using your transformational product. Not just a test of clicks but a feedback loop of conversations with people who are highly committed to overcoming the problem you solve. Not having a feedback loop ensures that you will be stuck and have absolutely no idea why your product is not selling. Validation and conversation also build trust. Would you rather spend time with people who care about your wants and needs? Or would you rather spend time with people who just want to sell you something and don't care about what you really want and need to be successful? The answer is probably obvious to you.

That doesn't mean the answer is obvious to everyone. A couple months ago, one of my favorite clients called and she was angry. She called to vent about a phone call she had with a so-called "guru." She related that the man never asked about where she was struggling or what she needed. He talked for twenty minutes about how his product would help her and tried to get her to purchase. She was angry because she set time aside in her busy calendar and was treated poorly. The man didn't want to know anything about her or her business. There was no validation or trust-building on his part at all. The result? She not only did not purchase, it is safe to say she will never speak to him again.

Your digital presence is used to act as "digital" listening, not sales. When you define the success principles of what you teach or sell and ask people to self- assess their skill set against what success looks like, you are allowing them to discover that they have a skill gap between where they are today and where they need to be to achieve the goals and success they are looking for. This is also a validation point for your business.

If you set up an assessment tool that allows your audience to assess their skill set versus success principles, you will allow for growth in a couple different areas:

1. The person assessing themselves will discover there is a skill gap that exists. They now know that they need some additional training.
2. This allows you as the business owner to identify recurring patterns in your audience. Where are they telling you they are struggling? If you lead them to conversations, you will find the exact words that they consistently use to describe the skill gap. Reflecting those words back to them in copy will resonate with them.
3. You will be able to separate the people who will pay for this product/ service and begin to identify patterns of be-havior that will allow you to refine your avatar and replicate and be in front of more of the same people.
4. The more your consumers give you feedback, the more you can help them.

If you are new, you are probably asking, how do I do that? You start by defining what you are selling and setting the standard of what success looks like. As a publisher, when authors bring me books, I want to know if they have a following. If they want to make a legit bestseller list (not Amazon), they need a significant email list and an actively-engaged social media following. They also need a sales funnel to lead their potential buyers to the prod-uct. As a company, we have them self-assess where they are at in different categories. We want to know what their social media following looks like. If you have a successful social media presence, you have active, engaged followers. Engagement means that your audience is liking, sharing, and commenting. You also have this social media audience transitioned into your email list. This is a huge piece that most entrepreneurs don't do. We are all one algorithm away from losing an audience we may have taken years to cultivate. Your email list ensures that does not happen. Asking questions and having your potential clients self-assess allows them to discover that they need you instead of you just telling them that they need you. You have also just discovered that your audience is willing to pay for that or maybe they are not.

Many years ago, I had a huge following on Google Plus. I gave them tips on how to be successful at publishing. When I used my first self-reflective quiz and asked some tough questions, I found out that I was working with an audience that had no money to invest in learning how to market a book successfully. These starving artists were never going to step up and publish and market a book. Most of them told me "they just wanted to write and have a bestseller." I closed that group within a week and went to locate my audience that would help me grow my business.

There are other areas that you can validate. By taking your program and defining the success principles, you can also validate your course delivery. Many years ago, I was part of a speaker's program that had a weekly call and one-on-ones with the speaking guru. I found out very quickly that the weekly call was a critique of speaker's sheets with a sprinkling of training mixed in. I soon lost interest because there was one training call a month and three critique calls. I wanted to be trained! When I inquired about the one-on-one calls that I purchased with this $12,000 program, I found out that it was fifteen minutes every quarter. Literally enough time to get hello's out of the way and she had to move to her next call. At the end of the program, her team reached out to me for a testimonial and I declined. I did not learn what was promised in the sales material of the program. Her big, juicy promise was not fulfilled.

What that lesson taught me (besides vowing to never hire another guru again) was that I needed to be focused on talking to potential clients and clients to find out how they wanted programs delivered to maximize the experience. This has been an important element in gaining referrals from my past clients. If you deliver and they get results, people will recommend you over and over.

Find out more about quizzes and how to use them: https://superbrandpublishing.com/getting-to-know-your-ideal-clients-through-a-quiz/

CHAPTER 4

BUILDING YOUR AVATAR

I n the beginning, your avatar is a guess. You think you might know who your product is perfect for but until it is validated you are estimating.

Many marketers will suggest key words as a way to validate. Until you talk to real people who are interested in your product or service, keywords are probably meaningless. There are two big mistakes that most entrepreneurs make with regard to understanding their ideal client.

The first is that their product is for everyone. You need to find the niche for your product. There are rarely products that are out there that are for everyone. A few years ago, a psychologist brought a program for happiness to our company. She insisted that everyone wanted to be happy. The sad truth is that some people thrive in their unhappiness. They hold onto their unhappiness because it is serving them in some way. The marketing that was needed for this product needed to be aimed at a smaller audience. We tested it in two different niches and found that her best market was women, 45-60 who had children leaving home and needed support in making shifts in their life. We did this by asking questions related to this experience and allowing the women who took the quiz we prepared to self- identify what was going on, and then following up with conversations. The program shifted from a "happiness program" to a "get clarity" program.

The second mistake is not talking to your ideal audience. By talking, I don't mean that they follow you on social media and you post to them. I mean actual talking and having a conversation with your ideal clients about what they want and need. Listening to the "buzz" words they are using to describe what they are going through. Many marketers call these "pain points."

Pain points are necessary for good copy. The mistake that is made around pain points is twofold. Your pain points must be tangible so the person who is experiencing the pain recognizes themselves in your pain point words and it must be communicated in an emotional way. Healers have difficulty articulating pain points because of the esoteric nature of their work. Translating an esoteric concept into an emotional communication helps your potential buyer feel like you are talking to them. Many first-time online marketers attempt to write their own copy and do not understand these points. The result is copy that has no emotional connection and falls flat.

It is essential that you build your avatar in-depth profile of who your ideal client is. The more you know your ideal consumer, the more of these people you will attract to you because you know them inside and out and are speaking their language. The first place to begin is with demographics. Demographics are the study of who your consumers are. To build a demographic profile, you must look at the following:

- Gender
- Age
- Location
- Income
- Marital Status
- Children (in some cases)

The next piece of building an avatar is building the psychographic profile. Building this profile informs about what your consumer does. In order to find out why your consumers purchase, you first must know what their behaviors are. Psychographics include but are not limited to:

- Opinions and behaviors
- Hobbies, activities, and interests
- Publications, associations, events
- Social media platforms and groups
- Experts they follow
- Dreams, aspirations, fears, pain points, goals/desires

It's Your Turn Now!

Describe the demographics of your ideal consumer:

Describe the psychographics of your ideal consumer in detail:

What areas of this new profile are validated by previous research and consumer connection?

What areas of this new profile are not validated by previous research and consumer connection?

Do you have a plan for validation?

Understanding Spending Behavior

This is the avatar piece that most marketers do not address... why does your ideal client purchase? This is the emotional piece of the puzzle. When you understand this, your marketing will be far more effective than it is without this. When planning a campaign, the creative aspect will only get you so far. You also need to understand what drives buying behavior so you can direct the decision to purchase. Most marketers lead potential clients and readers down a path without a clear understanding of what propels people to buy. This creates a situation where the marketer feels powerless.

Tony Robbins has talked about the six "basic need states" that drive every buyer to a purchase. By knowing what these need states are and which apply directly to your target audience, you are able to create a powerful marketing funnel and closing that speaks directly to those needs. Every person has all six needs in their world. Your job is to identify which need is consistently at the top of the list for your audience.

These Six Need States are:

1. Significance: *The need to be needed.* Marketing in this way requires that the buyer have the need to be significant and noticed. This is used extensively in ad campaigns that are targeted at self- image, like perfume, cars, clothes, beauty.
2. Connection: *The need to belong.* Ever seen an ad for weight loss or love? These are just two of the desires that connection ads target. Ads that fall under this category would be beer and dating.

3. Growth: *The need to be happy.* This is about experiences and learning. Gaining an awareness of self and rewarding others.

4. Contribution: *The need to be involved.* This is the need to make a difference in the world. Getting a promotion, recognition of achievement, and being able to give something back. The United Way ads are a perfect example of this. Football players giving back to the community. Help us help them.

5. Certainty: *The need to be sure.* This is used by products that sell any risk- based decisions. Investment institutions and insurance companies use this.

6. Variety: *The need for change.* Expanding your horizons. This is used by products in the luxury good and travel industries.

People are always surprised that beer commercials fall under the category of connection. Think about the ad for your favorite beer. There are always happy people connecting with other happy people. Would you be inclined to purchase a beer from an ad where a lone guy who hasn't showered in days is sitting in front of his TV, surrounded by empty food boxes and empty beer bottles? Me neither.

This is important to the type of product you are selling and how you show up. We hear so many coaches in the world talk about the impact they want to make and yet they are showing up with "significance" marketing instead of "contribution" marketing. The difference between the two is the emphasis on Influencer versus Impactor; being seen as opposed to making a difference. This can be a disconnect for people who are looking to be involved but not the face of the project.

Now It's Your Turn!

Answer these questions about your readers need states. Let this exercise flow freely and write what comes to mind first.

- What does your consumer's life look like before they buy your product?

- What will your consumer's life look like after they buy your product?

- What will NOT buying your product do for the consumer? What would that outcome look like?

- List your need states in the order which fits into your values.

- Which need state (s) is the primary reason that consumers will purchase your product? If you don't know, are there questions you could pose in an assessment to find out?

- What are the needs of your consumers? Have you asked your potential consumers what their needs are or are you guessing?

- What sort of transformation from needs to need states is necessary to drive your desired outcome? Example:

Your consumer's need state is significance and you are a relationship coach. How can your product make your consumer feel loved, special, and important?

- Listen to this Promote, Profit Publish episode on Spending Behavior: https://superbrandpublishing.com/the-six-core-human-needs-what-marketing-lacks-these-days/

CHAPTER 5

BUILDING EMOTIONAL CONNECTION

There are shifts that need to occur to build connection with your audience in a meaningful way. Now that you have your preliminary avatar built, it is time to understand what it is that these people want and need.

This is where authority marketing comes in. You need to position yourself as the solution to the problem that your avatar is experiencing. Niche marketing is the answer. Your job is to become a micro-celebrity in a field where no one else has the solution. You become the ONLY solution for a group of people who need what you have to offer. Some people find it scary to niche down a market. Mostly these are people who do not thoroughly understand that marketing to everyone means you are marketing to no one.

A psychologist once brought us a communication game. It was a cool game and she sunk about $30,000 into developing the board, dice, cards, and the outside packaging. Her problem was that she could not get people to purchase the game. Every time she mentioned communication, people ran. We ran a focus test and had people come in and play the game. Everyone had fun but no one said they would take it home and play it. The best feedback we got is that it would make a "great drinking game." That was not the right audience for a person who works at minimizing dysfunction. The worst feedback was that the game was a lot of work. People felt shy about answering questions about their morals and values. The entrepreneur decided not to take the project any further. She sold the games she had at her office and gave up. What would have been better was to mock-up the game and get feedback before she spent all of the money having it created.

So, how do you craft a messaging that makes you stand out from the crowd? There are three considerations that must be covered:

Pain Points:

Most people treat this like a laundry list with no emotional connection to what are the frustrations that are propelling your client's into action. What is the sticking point in their lives that is making them feel like they can't move forward? This is crucial and where speaking to your audience and seeing patterns will create the best connection.

Benefits:

What are the goals of your audience. What is the end- game that they are looking for? People want results. They want tangible results. Weight loss is a great example of this. If I see that my friend Jenny lost two pant sizes from working with a personal trainer, I have a visual of the tangible results.

Speaking to Your Audience

Language matters. When speaking to your audience, it is important to speak to them where they are at today. If you speak to them in a manner that is "over their heads," they feel overwhelmed and may not purchase. If you "talk down to them," they may decide that you are not qualified for the growth that they are trying to achieve. This is one of the opportunities of talking to people and seeing patterns; you understand how to talk to a beginner, someone who is a little more advanced, and someone who is advanced in the topic you teach. Speaking to a person in an enrollment conversation based on where they are today instead of where you think they should be, is the difference between closing a sale and not closing a sale.

Here is an example of messaging that works.

Goals   - My audience wants to make meaningful connections.

Dreams   - Connections that strive to be seen, loved, and admired by others

Pain Points - Never feeling liked or accepted by others. Feelings of unworthiness

Message   - I help caring, wonderful people who have feelings of unworthiness, create better connection and relationships in their lives.

It's Your Turn Now

1. What are your client's biggest goals or desires?

2. What are your client's hopes and dreams?

3. What are your client's pain points?

CHAPTER 6

PLATFORMS MATTER

W here are you being distributed? Is there engagement? These are key questions for most entrepreneurs. For years, social media and digital experts have been extolling the value of likes and shares. The problem with that is that likes and shares do not sell products. Engagement on social media and in person is the difference between talking at someone and talking to someone. This is okay when you are using a personal page. When you are posting in a business page or in a community, the goal is to have a conversation.

There are four big mistakes that business owners make in the online world:

1. Being on the wrong platform for your product/service.
2. Posting the wrong types of content for the platform audience.
3. Talking at people instead of talking to them.
4. Going in for a sale without building a real relationship.

Are you on the right social media platform for your product/service? The disconnect here is that most business owners are on the platform that they feel most comfortable using, not the platform that their ideal clients are using. If you are comfortable using Facebook and your potential clients are on LinkedIn, that is a problem.

A couple years ago, a woman brought me a program that addressed moving from a solopreneur to being a CEO and delegating. This seemed like a program that a lot of people in the entrepreneur space could use. This was an entrepreneur who designed the program that she needed because she lost a previous business by not addressing this problem. She wasn't attracting the right women to her program. The problem was that her program was for people who were on LinkedIn, not Facebook. No matter what she did on Facebook, she got a random sale here and there. Finally, after starting to build an audience on LinkedIn and adjusting her message, she was able to create a steady stream of clients. On Facebook she was looking for "badass" women. On LinkedIn, her message became more professional and women responded.

Posting the content that is wrong for the platform: each social media platform has a purpose and posting is different. Even the optimal times and dates vary from platform to platform. One of the big disconnects is posting the same content on all platforms. Even bigger mistake? Not understanding the audience variables from platform to platform and posting the same content. Here is a great example that I see over and over.

A local real estate agent is active on social media and feels that "authentic" means "overshare" about everything. This is another common mistake. She constantly posts about her ex-husband and their court trials. First of all, this is inappropriate social media fodder when you have a business. On Facebook she has a large following and after she demonizes her ex, a multitude of women jump on to commiserate with her. My first thought is always, "Wow, who would hire her? It doesn't seem like she has much time to provide great service with so much personal drama."

But wait….it gets better! She posts exactly the same things on LinkedIn. LinkedIn is a professional site filled with articles about business and business growth. There is absolutely no place for this on a business platform.

The posts that are right for LinkedIn are articles, podcasts, videos, and anything else related to your particular industry. LinkedIn is also a platform where people log in periodically. Posting more than twice a week does not make much sense. Facebook, Instagram, and Twitter are platforms where people are in and out all day. The point is that you need to learn the platform where your ideal audience is, not use the one that you are comfortable with and hope they find you.

Another problem is talking at people instead of talking to them. Talking to them is starting a conversation. Talking at them is just posting and hoping someone will engage. Good content starts conversations and builds trust. Many entrepreneurs do not create content because it takes too much time. Here's the deal… in the writing world, we talk about show, not tell. This means that you show how something looks, not tell how something works. This is a powerful way to communicate and the most difficult aspect of writing. Ask any writing coach! It is powerful because a picture is being painted. The same is true in the content world. Showing people in your content communication builds trust because you are showing people that you really do have the expertise you claim to have. When you just tell people, they don't know if you are for real or not. Look around in the real estate world. How many agents say things like, "I have been in the business for over 50 years." That implies that this person knows what they are doing. But if you really dig deep…does that mean that they have worked part-time and sold a house a year or have they sold fifty houses a year for the last fifty years and they are really good at what they do?

Some of the mistakes that business owners make that kill their engagement are listed below. You need to STOP these now!

1. Posting memes
2. Posting inspirational quotes

Here is why: none of these invite conversation. Memes may be funny or make a point, but in the end, no one remembers you. They may remember the meme but do not attribute it to you. Inspirational quotes are nice, but they are not memorable. You are like everyone else out there in the noise that is social media. People who do not have a platform built around their brand and their message and post quotes from others because they do not have their own content. You may get likes and shares, which are social proof. However, if you aren't getting pocketbook proof, it is not working.

I always like to use dating as an analogy to marketing. Imagine if you went out on a first date and your date took you to a nice restaurant. A half hour into the meal, your date proposes marriage. You don't really know this person and are shocked that now he or she wants to spend the rest of your lives together. In other words, this person is trying to sell you on togetherness. I don't know about you, but I would start looking around for the restroom and hoping the back door was nearby so I could hop in an Uber and go home! That's exactly what it feels like when you try to sell a product before having a relationship.

Selling before you build a relationship is SPAM. Sorry that was so harsh, but that is exactly how people see it. Business owners with a platform and a marketing funnel do not need to sell prematurely. In fact, most of the time, they do not need to sell at all because they have a client base of people who know, like, and trust them.

There is nothing worse than accepting a friend request only to find a salesy message in your inbox. Relationship building is key to high-ticket sales. Most of the time, if someone is willing to pay for a high-ticket program, it is because they know who you are and the value you provide. People are literally buying YOU! No one, and I mean no one clicks on a program that is over $997. Even a program at that price point requires conversation most of the time. So just say no to people who practice SPAM online.

About three years ago, a man reached out to me on Facebook Messenger to wish me a happy birthday. I barely knew him, and he wrote a nice note. When I thanked him, BOOM! There is was... the sales pitch. He does it every year. The same happy birthday greeting, followed by the same pitch. He lives in the same town I do and when I see him...I literally hide. The lesson here is that you don't do anything online that you wouldn't do in person. Could you imagine if someone wished you happy birthday in person and then proceeded with a sales pitch?

Before you post a single word about your business or on social media, your foundation needs to be in place. Your business credibility is on the line. Before you embark on any social media posting on behalf of your business, four key pieces of your platform MUST be in place:

1. Your narrowed target audience
2. Your message
3. Branding
4. High value, service-driven content

There are other factors that will help you get your message out on your ideal platform.

Consistency:

This is where many marketers fail. Potential clients are confused because messaging is not consistent. Consistent messaging across all platforms helps people understand who you are and what your message is all about. You want to use the same message over and over to reiterate your message and be understood. Consumers receive a lot of messages and may only be tuned in some of the time. By staying consistent, you have more potential to get your message through.

A poor platform, in many places provides a venue for consumer overload. There is so much content out in the Internet world that it can be mind-boggling to look at! Combine that with the fact that attention spans are shrinking, and it can be increasingly difficult to catch and keep anyone's attention. In addition to keeping your message consistent, it is important to keep it simple. Narrowing down your message and keeping your focus and words succinct will help. Use plain language and short words. Get to the point and make a statement!

Visual Appeal:

Every platform is changing its display capacity to become more visually appealing. With the growing success of sites like Pinterest, social media sites have caught on to the actions of consumers. As consumers scroll through timelines, they receive hundreds of messages. The messages that provide the most engagement are those with bold images. Determine what images are in line with your brand and consistently promote those images to your audiences. In addition to bold images, consistent branding must be a key image in the repetitive mix that is necessary to keep the consumer's attention. Here is where the caution comes in with images. Many entrepreneurs try to save money by making their own graphics with something like Canva. Unless you are really good at this, you should delegate graphics to someone else. Your business is competing with many great marketers. Graphics that are out of proportion don't help move your brand forward, they just look like poorly-created graphics. Invest in someone who can create outstanding visual experiences.

Differentiation:

Make your brand and your platform stand out! So many business owners try to emulate others instead of creating their own. Brand loyalty and patronage are the keys to returning to your business. Consumers consistently stay with recognizable brands regardless of price or convenience. This means if you copy a recognizable brand, people will go to the brand they recognize, not yours!

Without fail, when clients come to me with marketing funnels, there are mistakes which are repeated over and over.

1. The business has not built an avatar of their ideal client.
2. No message clarity.
3. No "I am factor" in branding.
4. Posting on social media before avatar, message, branding, and content development have been created.

At the end of the day, the followers DO NOT belong to you. If you are on Facebook, they belong to Mark Zuckerberg or whoever owns the platform. The reason that engagement is so crucial is that the focus needs to be to build confidence and trust on social media and transition that trust into your marketing funnels.

Building Your Funnel Intentionally

The single most important factor of an intentional build is that people want to be there and build a relationship. The digital marketing age has sparked a value crisis. For the last few years, entrepreneurs have been giving away free information in a way that was one-sided. The value creation was established in the sense that "I will now give you free stuff and you will buy from me because I created value." The truth of this is that most people opted-in just to get the free stuff. They had no interest in ever hiring the person they got the free stuff from.

After our webinars, we would send out an email to the people who did not purchase. We heard a lot about how business owners were going from webinar to webinar to webinar so that they could figure out how to piece the information together and not hire anyone. They actually told us that! The crazy part of all of this is that if you were coached by a webinar expert, you know that you deliver a webinar in a way that is not designed to be able to piece together the info. Good webinar strategy gives enough to "get excited" but not enough for a DIY platform builder to create on their own.

One of the biggest traffic builders that is promoted is Facebook advertising. Facebook started out with a terrific targeting platform. Over time, as the consumer shifted and stopped clicking on ads, this method of gathering an audience has withered on the vine. The biggest problem for coaches trying to sell programs is that there is no physical product. Facebook and Google ads are far more effective when there is a physical product.

The second problem that Facebook ads created was an avenue for artificial social proof. One of the big strategies that social media specialists engaged in with their clients was building a business page and driving traffic for social proof. The problem is that Facebook ads were appearing in front of low-value audiences. This means that the ten thousand people that were liking your page, were not opting-in to your content. This is low-value social proof.

When we were building an assessment funnel for one of my clients, she asked if we should share this with her Facebook group since it had over four thousand people in it. I was a little "wowed" that she had a group that large and was struggling with sales. When I queried further, she shared that her previous coach had her run Facebook ads into the group.

The moral of this story is that it is not about the quantity of followers that you have, it is the quality. One of my clients speaks regularly to small groups of entrepreneurs. Speaking once a week to a group of 20-30 people is garnering her about four sales conversations a week with about two closes. Eight closes a month at a price point of two thousand dollars a program, is creating a decent income. The bonus is coming from the people who weren't quite ready that she is nurturing. One or two of them are purchasing as well. That is what we are looking for with intentional traffic, interested people who are creating a steady income for us.

Now It's Your Turn!

Review your social media over the last six months. This exercise is not meant for you to beat yourself about the way you have been posting. It is to merely make you aware of how you are appearing online. Write it down and let it go. Consider the following questions:

1. Where are you posting? Business, personal, community?

2. Is the platform you are posting on audience appropriate?

3. What are you posting?

4. How often do you post?

5. What does the engagement look like? Are people commenting on your posts?

6. Are you building relationships and transitioning those people into the funnel?

7. Do you need to get training in order to convert social proof to pocketbook proof?

CHAPTER 7

VALIDATING YOUR IDEA AND YOUR AUDIENCE

I magine a world where you create a product that doesn't have a buyer, or a book that doesn't have a reader. Does that make sense to you? Believe it or not, that is where most authors and entrepreneurs get stuck in their thinking. They have an "if I create it, they will come" mentality.

The sad fact is that "they" won't show up. The result? Your book, product, or service goes nowhere, and you feel like a failure.

Every good product starts with *a problem that is being solved.* You may be viewing your book, product, or service as an avenue to visibility, but the hard, cold truth is this: without a clearly identified audience, your product becomes just another failed attempt.

What this means to you, as a product developer, is that you have to test your market and your solution before you write your book, create your program, or market consulting packages. But even more immediate, you have to know who your audience is so you can test your solution.

Just like a well-written book, your solution needs to be crafted and tested in a way that shows your ideal client they need it, not tell them they need it. The frustrations they are feeling need to be self-assessed and embraced by your ideal consumer.

In the area of self-help, people have to decide for themselves that they are ready to solve their problem. No amount of marketing will convince them that they have a problem. Consider this for a moment: have you ever played golf or another sport with your significant other and he/she is trying to coach you and TELL you what to do? Most people who just said yes are probably re-living the frustration that is felt when you are TOLD what to do. The same applies here. This is why it is so important for your solution to contain an element of emotion in the presentation of the problem.

Why is My Audience Not Responding?

This is a question that I hear from entrepreneurs all day long. Most authors, coaches, and speakers create products before they find out who their audience is and what that audience wants. It is the way the coaching model has presented itself. You have an area of expertise, go to a business conference and immediately you are sold programs to teach you how to speak, how to write a book, how to market, and how to set up programs. Suddenly you are $200,000 in debt without a sustainable business. The model is horrible. If you had taken your brilliant idea to investors to get funding, they would want your product and audience validated before they gave you money. Unfortunately, many coaches bootstrap themselves into bankruptcy because they follow the hype of the coaching business model.

Most new entrepreneurs are reading books to get started. They don't understand that our consumers become savvier about digital marketing every day, which means that the market and how to connect with them is shifting as well. New entrepreneurs who are do-it-yourselfers also don't realize that they are competing with very savvy marketers. Your potential clients can spot amateur marketing efforts a mile away. The way we market online shifts about every nine months. What that means to the business owner is that what worked last year, doesn't work today. Case in point: in 2015, webinars became popular and everyone had one with a sales pitch at the end. In 2019, the people who are showing up to webinars are mostly warm traffic. They have been referred by someone who has used the product, or they have been following the influencer for a while. This makes using a Facebook or Google ad to drive traffic (which is mostly cold traffic) a futile effort. People are exhausted from the Joint Venture emails, webinars, and emails. What they are looking for is personal connection and relationship building. The coaching industry hates this because their selling point has been lifestyle. It is a great lifestyle, but you must have a sustainable business before you get the "lifestyle." Because of these market shifts, most new coaches, authors, and speakers are reading books to get them started that have obsolete information. What they really need is to define their offer and then set the success principles in a way that they can present to an audience and find out where they are in relationship to success.

Building your brand depends on building your brand with a receptive audience. Most consumers have a tough time with this aspect of engagement because they failed to market to a particular niche. Without knowing who your audience is, product development is almost sure to lead to failure. Finding an audience after your product is developed can be an almost impossible task. This leads to a helter-skelter approach to consumer engagement that leaves business owners frustrated. They work with the wrong platforms and expend wasted time and energy trying to force or buy engagement. This approach is like trying to hammer a square peg into a round hole.

The key to knowing with which platform your people resonate depends on you taking a deep dive into where your people are and what they resonate with and need. One of the big failures my company sees over and over are people who write a book because someone told them that their product or service wasn't selling because no one knew who they were. In a sense, that is true. The problem is that a book is not the "magic bullet." In most cases it becomes another failed product because the author really doesn't know who their audience is.

Here are some ways that Assessment Marketing helps:

The Discovery Process:

Find out what people want before you create products and services. If there is one thing that becomes apparent after many people take your assessment, it is the patterns that are revealed. When you have 4 or 5 categories of questions surrounding what you teach and you begin to analyze the answers, patterns emerge. One section that has poor answers in almost every assessment I have is the knowledge my consumers have about funnels. Consumers know nothing about conversion or setting up a funnel that connects. Even worse? They do not understand that their consumers become more and more savvy every day and that what worked to convert a lead into a client in 2016, probably isn't effective now.

Using assessment helps in the following ways:

1. New Markets
2. Existing Markets

3. New Products
4. Existing Products

New markets can be explored using an assessment in front of different audiences. One thing that large companies do consistently well is market research. For smaller companies or solopreneurs, market research can be outside of their budget. A good marketing research firm is expensive. But there's hope! Using the assessment marketing gives you feedback about your ideal consumer and information that you probably didn't realize. In marketing, the more you know your consumer, the better your product will sell. Knowing your consumer spending habits and behaviors is essential.

One of the challenges for people writing books is that they seek an audience after it is completed. The easy part of publishing is writing and publishing a book. Most people won't put the time into audience building while they are writing the book. I have always had a difficult time communicating that to people who bring books to our publishing company. It's not that we aren't communicating to our authors; it's that they are not receptive to the message. Most authors become disillusioned by the publishing process when the book fails. When we started using the assessments for potential authors, we began to see patterns in what was in place to build a platform and what wasn't. Our publishing packages were revamped to include platform building. The packages were sold at a higher price point and we did not take on anyone who just wanted to publish. At first, we thought this would be risky. It turned out to generate more revenue. Now we were only taking on serious authors. _Listening_ was the key. You can consider an assessment a form of "digital listening."

This leads to _audience validation_. If you were a start-up who was out seeking venture capital for your business, your potential investors would want you to prove that you have validated your audience. Most small businesses don't do this well.

Audience validation can include:

1. Finding out if your audience is the best audience to pursue.
2. Determining if a new market is worth pursuing.
3. Eliminating or minimizing risk.
4. Proceeding with confidence.

In other words, are you speaking to the right audience about the right product for them? I was at an inventor's event and there was a gentleman who was asking a group of men about a part that he invented that allowed the toilet seat to be cleaned under the back side where most of the germs reside and is inaccessible to clean. His pitch to these men was that the part was easy to install. According to Girl Power Marketing, 85% of consumer home goods are purchased by women. While men seemed ambivalent about the toilet part and how easy it was to install, the women who were shown the part were much more excited. Women are typically the germ patrol in any household. The women who realized that this part would allow them to clean the area that was awful from a particular gender (sorry boys!) missing the toilet bowl, they were excited. This gentleman quickly realized that he was promoting in front of the wrong audience.

Existing markets can be queried with assessments to find out what they really want from you. This can be done by sending out an assessment to your existing Facebook group or your email list. What we often find from this experience is that the commitment section of the quiz is revealing.

When we get brave and drill down on the right questions:

1. Do you want to solve the problem?

2. Are you willing to invest the time and money necessary to fix the problem?
3. Would you value time with me to see what is possible?

When we ask these questions, we often find that we have an audience full of people who opted in for the free stuff! My clients find that they have wasted a lot of time and money trying to convince people with no money that they need to hire them. This is the time to take control back of your income producing activities and start spending time with motivated people who do have the money to hire you.

Using assessments with existing markets:

1. Identifies top challenges.
2. Locates underserved or ignored markets.
3. Determines if there is a soft "underbelly" in your market.

As mentioned above, many times we are chasing people with no money. I have mentioned my Google Plus group. I had huge following on Google Plus. After a year of courting these people, I realized that I wasted a year convincing a group of starving artists that they needed me. When I used the assessments to find out more about my audience and who was willing to pay, I began to see patterns developing that made prospecting more consistent. The patterns showed me a profile of who was consistently purchasing.

New products can be beta-tested, and the consumer can give you the feedback you need to sell the product or revamp the product. Having a connection to your audience that allows for feedback is critical. If you listen closely, you will hear the language that the consumer is using with you. If you hear a language pattern over and over, use these terms to reflect back to the consumer in your copy.

New product assessments can identify:

1. The best new product to pursue.
2. Determine if there is a market for your new product.
3. Calculate the success probability and position marketing strategies before you invest in production.

Existing products can be beta-tested as well. We know for example, that downloadable programs that used to sell well are not selling like they used to. We frequently get calls from people who want to set up the "cash machine." The highly touted "make money while you sleep" products. My company performed a study in 2017 and learned that people no longer purchased these programs for a couple of reasons. First and foremost, the consumer did not finish the program. Secondly, if they got stuck, there wasn't a mentor to help them. What we learned from this study was that consumers wanted programs where the mentor worked alongside of them instead of overwhelming them with information. As a result of the study, we began re-purposing some of the programs our clients created into experiential programs. Our clients used the assessments to validate this premise and re-introduce their programs in a different format. This was a win-win for everyone. Our clients generated more revenue with less clients because of the added experiential component. The success rate of their clients also increased. More happy clients translated into more referrals and revenue. Let

Assessments can be used with existing products to:

1. Determine why consumers are not purchasing.

2. Identify a missing piece that would entice consumers to purchase.

3. Capitalize on overlooked product opportunities (like adding experiential learning).

The bottom line is that you are looking for what it will take for consumers to purchase.

A key piece to validating is laying out your program in outline form and defining the success principles before you build and spend time and money. When you lay out what it looks like to achieve success in your program and ask questions in a self-reflective way, people understand that they are not doing what it takes to be successful at what they are trying to achieve. If the questions are penned correctly, the person taking your assessment will know by the end of the assessment that there are gaps and they need to engage you to find out more. When a prospect comes to the table or enrollment call already knowing they need you, it takes the "salesy" feeling out of the call.

The wording of the assessment statement is crucial to the self-assessment process. Often, we word assessment questions in a detached way. To have your prospect connect emotionally, it is imperative to phrase with "I or my" in each statement if the assessment subject pertains to individual achievement.

Learn more about validation and consumer research in ur Promote, Profit, Publish episode with Market Research expert Laura Hazzard: https://superbrandpublishing.com/consumer-research-through-focus-groups-with-laura-hazzard/

Connecting Success with Emotion

Your solution is the third foundational piece that you need to create before you begin testing. Before we begin creating products for a solution, which can be time-consuming and expensive, we need a blueprint or plan. This will minimize the overwhelm you feel in creating and provide a plan for potential consumers.

Before we get started on the laying out your blueprint, let's chat about the feelings that your consumers are experiencing. For most people who are ready to solve a problem, they are overwhelmed by what is creating the problem. What that means to you is that you have to cut through that overwhelm and lead them to a point where they know that you are the solution they have been looking for. The first point in this process is creating an outline of your solution. In an organized fashion, lay it all out on paper and follow the points from A to B to C and make sure that they make logical sense. When you present to your ideal audience, if it doesn't make sense, they will disconnect immediately.

After this is all laid out on paper, make sure that you are giving people a logical pathway to what they want. Do not get caught up in a culture of random products. This is the best way to destroy your brand. Create a logical pathway to the solution. For example, if your ideal client wants to learn to set stronger boundaries to create a happier life, create a pathway that gets them there and deals with the emotional fallout of change. What creates confusion for your clients is when you get struck in communicating your process. No one cares about the process to get from point A to point B! You may have the best, most ingenious process on the planet but your clients want to know about the results.

After you have laid this out on paper and created a solution, go back to each module/ lesson/ step and start testing objections.

This will be key in your marketing efforts. The process looks something like this:

Lesson One: Creating a niche audience

1. What do people do instead of creating a niche audience?
2. What does it look like when they do not create a niche audience?
3. What does it feel like when they do not create a niche audience?
4. What happens to their results?
5. What does it look like when you follow your plan and create a niche audience?
6. What are the results when they do it your way?

Here is an example:

1. What do people do instead of creating a niche audience?

   They market to everyone and spend too much on marketing without results.

2. What does it look like when they do not create a niche audience?

   Results and sales seem random and they can't figure out how to achieve consistent sales.

3. What does it feel like when they do not create a niche audience?

   The business owner feels frustrated and overwhelmed.

4. What happens to their results?

   Sales are random and their business struggles.

5. What does it look like when you follow your plan and create a niche audience?

   The business owners know exactly who their ideal client is and spend their marketing dollars effectively.

6. What are the results when they do it your way?

   Sales becomes more effortless and revenue is consistent.

Why is this all important? Because, you want your audience to self-identify that what they are doing looks and feels the way that you are identifying as ineffective. You are showing them that what they are doing isn't working in an emotional way instead of telling them they are wrong.

When you follow this pathway for your solution, you are creating your marketing as you go along.

Now It's Your Turn

1. Create an outline for your solution.

2. Go through and detail what people do instead of your solution that keeps them stuck.

3. Go through the outline lesson by lesson and document the objections you hear over and over that keep people from overcoming the problem you solve.

4. Ask people who have this problem how this looks and feels for them when the problem is not being solved.

5. Use the six-step guideline above on every module to make sure you have all of the answers to the questions

CHAPTER 8

SERVING, NOT SELLING

Prequalification Serves Everyone

When I started my company, I brought one of the principles I learned from another career. When my children were small, I embarked on a career in real estate. Within a year of starting this new venture, I was one of the top producers in an office of 400 agents. Mostly, I can attribute that to knowing how to market. The one thing that was drilled into me was that I never put a buyer in my car until he is pre-qualified. This is difficult for most business owners to do, especially newer real estate agents, because they want so badly to sell something. Here's the deal: prequalification saves business owners time and money. It is truly the key to attracting and keeping the right clients.

A key factor to getting the right clients is asking the right questions to prequalify. When we build assessments for our clients, there is always a series of three questions that we use to determine if we want to talk to them. The first question is, "Do you want to solve the problem?" This sounds like a simple question but, for many business owners, your company may not be the solution, or they have other pressing priorities that need attention. This question will prequalify if there is any interest in your solution and if it is a top priority to solve now.

The second question is around the investment. I talk to coaches and small businesses with high-ticket products. The one complaint I hear over and over is that the people they are talking to can't afford them. As anyone who has had an enrollment conversation knows, this can be a challenge and take up a lot of time. By asking if your assessment taker is willing to "invest in a solution," you are basically asking if they can afford you. If the response is high, on a scale of one to ten, it is time to build a relationship. If it is not, keep in touch or let them go. There are people out there who will say, "If they really want this, they will go find the money." That is great. But do you really want to take on a client who has spent his last dime on your product and has put themselves in dire straits by working with you?

When I worked in the real estate world, agents would brag about how many leads they had. These same people rarely closed a deal. You can have 62 leads, but if they aren't prequalified, they are scraps of paper or dormant entries in your CRM. The only ones who will close the deal are those who are prescreened and have purchase power. Prequalification solves this problem and focuses on working with the clients who will purchase at some point.

The third prequalification question we ask is, "Would you value an appointment to discuss the possibilities?" This question also corresponds to a link in the autoresponder for a calendar. If the prospect is qualified, we want to build that relationship right away. This allows the prospect to set up an appointment. Because we have asked for email and phone number for the prospect to receive their results, it now gives our sales team an opportunity to set an appointment if the prospect does not set one right away. This allows the relationship to begin with a conversation, not a click.

Prequalification serves everyone in the relationship. The business owner immediately knows which leads to work and the prospect gets more personal attention and relationship building because the business owner is not wasting time chasing people who are not interested. It is a win-win for everyone. Here is a real-life example. Dan Clark, a professional speaker and co-creator of the *Chicken Soup for the Soul* series, used this methodology from the stage. He had people take out their phones in a room of about seventy people. His assessment was a 2-3 minute experience that asked the people in the room to self-assess where they were in alignment with the success principles laid out in his program that taught how to become a paid speaker. Out of seventy people in the room, sixty-one people took the assessment right there. This created three outcomes for Dan. One, he just captured the name, email address, and phone number of most of the room. Secondly, it created curiosity about the speech Dan was about to give. Thirdly, Dan just found out who in the room was interested in investing to become a paid speaker. Out of the sixty-one people who took the assessment, forty-eight identified that they wanted to solve the problem and were willing to invest. Of those forty-eight, fifteen people booked an appointment to have a half-hour consult with Dan. After the event, Dan's team reached out to the high-commitment prospects who did not book an appointment and set up time with Dan. There were even a couple of people who tried to buy the low-cost program that was listed on the thank you page without booking an appointment.

The point of all of this was to create more conversations and the opportunity to build relationships. Some people were sold on the initial consult and others needed a little more time. This is how prequalification works, spending your time with the right people who already know that they need you.

CHAPTER 9

OVERCOMING THE "CLICK" MENTALITY

I n the last few years, many of the digital marketing companies popped up overnight and give you a blah...blah...blah story about the advertising that will make you a star in about a year and after you've dumped about $50,000 into it....maybe we'll know after the first $50k if we need more. They tell you great stories like.... we are getting a thousand clicks! You are excited about that thousand clicks until you have to make your car payment. "Hello, Lexus, can I make my payment with clicks this month?" If this works for you...please create a coaching program and teach the rest of us how to pay the bills with unconverted clicks! The problem is that everyone believes the hype until they don't get results. My company hears stories every day from companies who are teetering on the edge of disaster because of a marketing company that did not deliver.

The tragic story starts like this.... they created a strategic marketing that looked pretty good. It had a neat message and the owner assured us that they had many happy clients. They agreed to create a campaign, gave us keywords that would be appropriate, ran ads and nothing. The first month was their "test." The test needed further validation, so we spent more money on ads the second month. They kept telling us "it's working, it's working," but we weren't seeing any results. We were doing all of these things that the company was recommending and by month six we knew we still weren't getting any ROI. In the case of many coaches, they weren't having people book appointments or show up at events. Thirty thousand dollars later, we were broke and still had marketing that wasn't hitting the mark. By the time we were done, we couldn't afford to hire another company.

This story is not atypical. Companies are trying to drive cold traffic through Google and Facebook ads and hoping that they will convert to sales. Business owners are not savvy enough to know that an "awareness campaign" is not going to give them instant gratification business. This is especially true if you are running ads on a product that is not a physical product. Business owners need a plan that creates conversion. If you are being told that it is "working" and you don't see sales, your marketing is not converting.

What Does Conversion Mean?

Conversion is accomplished by analyzing and adjusting the following:

- Your message: A strong, consistent message is one of the main keys to connection. Analytics will be able to tell you where your message is successful and where it isn't.
- Your medium: Choose the medium of delivery based on ease of production and consistency.
- Analytics on social media and your landing pages will tell a further story about your mediums and where your leads are coming from.

- How you are perceived- The analytics of what you said, where you said it, and how it was received by the audience. This is where you find out if your message is the pain-point solution that your audience is looking for or if you missed the mark!

- Campaign Planning is another element to successfully launching your book and your funnels. Each campaign that you launch will have its own message and digital assets/freebies. However, each campaign will need to have four objectives, in order to be successful:

  1. Awareness: This is where you have been building a combination of elements to create awareness of who you are, your brand, and the desired message that you want your audience to hear. In the marketing world, this is called "driving traffic." There are only four main avenues of driving traffic or broadcasting your campaign: email, social media, SEO (search engine optimization), and pay per click ads.

  2. Interest: The key is providing relevant content for your target audience. This is focused not only on the content/ digital asset that you are promising to deliver, but also in the aesthetics of the page you are using to opt-in or land on.

  3. Motivation: There must be motivation and a desire to change from the deliverable promise. The end game is book or program sales. If the potential reader arrives at the page, there must be more than just a page that is landed on and looked at. There must be enough motivation on that page to inspire the reader to take the next step, which is to click through and download the asset. This is also where the words or copywriting are essential

as well. The right key words and use of subtle sales techniques and language optimize conversion rates.

4. Closing: Every funnel needs a close! The end game is always to establish a relationship and lead consumers to buy. You must show the consumer what the desired action is that you are looking for. Do not assume that they will just figure it out. Spell it out!

Every step is an opportunity for analyzing your funnel. Awareness will bring clients to your funnel. The opt-in and landing pages will pique their interest. Your copywriting, graphics, and promise will provide motivation, and the endgame is the click to close. The good news is that if your funnel is not successfully converting to closing, you can use the analytics to figure out which step in the funnel is not resonating with your audience. The biggest funnel mistake business owners make is not looking at the analytics and determining where the consumer disconnect is happening.

Why Knowing Your Metrics Matters

You are what you post. Are you tired of hearing that from so-called social media and content experts? Of course, that is a given. What matters is not what you think you look like when you post. It is that old adage that "perception is reality." It is what others are perceiving from your posts. If you are scattered and all over the place like Dory, from *Finding Nemo*, that is how people perceive your business.

What does that mean? Feedback and analytics matter. You can't tell how people are responding to what you are saying on social media unless you understand traffic and look at the metrics.

When I work with entrepreneurs on platform-building and marketing funnels, three things stand out.

1. Many entrepreneurs have their platforms built by someone else and they don't know how to read analytics.
2. Many entrepreneurs have their marketing funnels built by someone else and they don't know how to read the analytics.
3. Entrepreneurs know little to nothing about traffic and so they do not understand what marketing and funnel experts are selling them.

Do you see a recurring theme?

So, let's talk a minute about what happens when you do not build a platform. In other words, when you do not have a target audience, a message, a brand, and content.

1. You spam "buy my product, buy my product."
2. You are annoying to people who are not interested.
3. You must have a huge ad spend because you are randomly trying to reach everyone and hoping for amazing results.

How does that look from a metrics standpoint? People like your posts, but no comments. No opt- in for your lead magnets, low email open rate, and few people show up for events and webinars. And the worst? No opportunities for conversations that lead to relationship building and enrollment conversations. Crickets... There is no place to go from there.

Service-driven content posting takes eyes off of you and points to value delivery and the consumer. When you are posting in a way that indicates "look at me," this is ego-driven. Ego-driven turns the conversation away from the consumer and onto the person delivering the message. In other words, it takes the focus away from your product. Consumers look at ego and money versus how the product can help them.

Service-driven content posting provides the following for the consumer:

1. Education/Value delivery
2. Trust-building between you and the consumer through active communication without selling
3. Establishing you as the expert with cutting-edge ideas and strategies

Service-driven content posting provides the entrepreneur with:

1. Feedback about audience/consumer and pain points.
2. Communication with potential consumers in a way which allows consumers to feel seen and heard.
3. List building anytime, anywhere.

Three Kinds of Traffic and How to Maximize Traffic

Every single post must provide value to your potential client. When planning a post, this is your first objective. The second objective is to begin a conversation. Before you can do this, you must understand the kind of traffic you are speaking to. This may mean that you have several campaigns running at the same time to segmented groups. The traffic type determines who you are talking to and how you are talking to them. Consider this…are you spending a lot of time trying to communicate ineffectively to traffic that is not yours?

That's what most entrepreneurs do. It is a time and effort waster because we are not speaking the right language to the right audience and our results become a mixed bag. We are trying to sell to cold traffic when we should be making them aware of our brand. The coaching industry runs into this problem a lot. Marketing companies run ads that invite cold traffic to a webinar and no one shows up.

There are three types of traffic online:

1. The traffic you control.
2. The traffic you don't control.
3. The traffic you own.

The traffic you control is the traffic that you run ads, solo banners, and affiliate links to. You target them and attempt to lead them into converting to the traffic you own. This traffic is expensive for the most part because it is also cold traffic. Cold traffic is comprised of people who are new to you. They do not know you, like you, or trust you yet. They are dipping their toes in the water to see if you can provide what they need.

The biggest mistake that marketers make with this type of traffic is that they sell too soon. This is fickle traffic at best. The quality of the new consumer depends on the quality of the ad targeting. If the ad targeting is generic or poor, you will get clicks that will never convert. Cold traffic requires nurture sequences and lots of warming up before a sale can occur.

Traffic you do not own is mystifying to most entrepreneurs because they thought they owned it. Social media, SEO, and Public Relations (PR) all fall into this category. The clearest example of this is social media. If you have a Facebook page, you do not own that traffic. Mark Zuckerberg owns that traffic. The tragic result of this is that when Mr. Zuckerberg and crew change an algorithm, you can lose an audience that you spent years cultivating.

Back in the days, when Facebook business pages where engagement places, one of my friends had a rocking Facebook page with over two thousand fully engaged writers and authors. When Facebook change the algorithms and decided that communities were the new engagement points, business owners lost visibility of the people who were on their business page unless they were personal friends. The result is that only 4-7% of the people on your business page actually see what you post. Our business pages have become nothing more than a credit card holder for ads. That was by- design because Facebook saw a way to create more ad revenue at the business owners expense.

The traffic you own is what business owners should strive to collect. This is your email list. Your email list is your gold and your hedge against algorithm changes and platforms disappearing. Many marketing firms will tell you that email lists are dead and no one is using them. Just like podcasting was vogue ten years ago and is now hot, marketing goes through trends. The beauty of your list is that no one can take it away from you. Always be in list-building mode.

Listen to this Promote, Profit, Publish episode on Traffic Temperature: https://superbrandpublishing.com/webinar-traffic-why-youre-getting-cold-warm-or-hot-traffic/

Real Relationships Require
Real Conversations

The beauty of assessment marketing is that it is a lead magnet/free gift that allows an exchange of information. Most lead magnets fail to convert because entrepreneurs don't understand what their audience wants and needs. The concept, whether it is an e-book or something else, takes a guess at what the consumer wants or needs.

There is no information about the consumer that comes back to the entrepreneur expect an email address with a name. There is no point of conversion for the entrepreneur to move forward with that will enhance future projects or create conversations. Imagine trying to build a relationship with another person without really knowing what their wants and needs are. That's what most lead magnets do.

The assessment gives you information that is critical to future projects. If you analyze the results carefully, you will find:

1. Patterns: You can tell which areas consumers are thriving in and where they are not. Not just on an individual basis but as a group.

2. Content Creation Becomes Easier: When you analyze the patterns of your consumers, you know exactly what content will benefit them and what will not.

3. What Level Your Audience is Performing: The answers to the micro- commitment section at the end can tell you who is responding to your content most often. This becomes the basis of niching down your audience and understanding where they are at in the process you teach.

4. Language: Once you know the level your audience is at and where they need help, your copywriting becomes easy. You know how to speak to your audience and where their pain points are at that level.

5. Selling Becomes Easy: Assessment takers already know, from their results, that they need you.

6. Your Messaging is Clear: By the time they are done with the quiz, they know exactly what you teach.

There are several places you can use the assessments within your funnel. They will be briefly covered in this chapter.

- Speaking from the Stage: Capture that audience in a powerful way that inspires trust and converts. Not only will you have names, addresses, and phone numbers... you will know exactly what that audience needs and how motivated they are to take next steps! Ask the audience to take out their phones and find out their skill gaps in 2-4 minutes. Have a slide deck available telling them what they will receive while taking the assessment. 2-4 minutes of silence from the stage can seem like an hour.

- List Building: Here's some news.... your job is to transition your social media audience over to your list so it is your own. We are all one algorithm change away from losing our life's work. Be sure that you have a tool that allows your Facebook group to tell you how motivated they are to work with you. My sense is that most people join groups and just sit there, never intending to engage or purchase. Many of these "joiners" are there because they want to self-promote.

- Pre-Live Event: Get your attendees crystal clear on where they are and what they need before attending your event. Wouldn't it be great to have your time at an event fully booked with qualified prospects before you even teach a single concept?

- Pre-Stage Marketing: Have your host's attendees take the assessment before arriving and call those high commitment takers and make appointments to talk to them at the event. Nothing is more powerful than a face-to-face meeting and you have the results to speak to them. This is the beginning of a more personal relationship.

- <u>Pre-Webinar Sequences</u>: Help attendees find out which pieces they are missing and how this webinar will fill those learning gaps. They will sign up and they will show up. The strategy is to send this out in the twenty-four hour reminder email.

- <u>List-Re-engagement</u>: Engage a non-responsive list by providing a tool that will identify what they need so you can create relevant free content to re- energize them.

- <u>Student Progress Sequences</u>: Help your clients discover how much they have learned by taking the assessment at the beginning and the end of every course. People who see results from your products and services, make great referral sources and leave glowing reviews.

- <u>Pre-Strategy Session Sequences</u>: Exponentially grow your sales conversions by talking to only qualified prospects who know they need you and are ready to invest.

- <u>Facebook and LinkedIn groups</u>: Social media groups made up of highly committed individuals create a more dynamic conversation. Pre-qualify members before you let them into your space. The right people will exponentially increase engagement (and therefore conversions) from your groups.

- <u>Podcasts, Radio, and YouTube Videos</u>- These are all stats that you do not own. The stats are owned by the platform. By inserting an assessment as an ad or a shout-out within the program, you can begin to turn your followers into clients.

- <u>Books</u>- This is another area where you have access to stats, but not details about who is purchasing. By adding an assessment in the front of the book to gauge skill before your information and adding again at the end, you have lead capture from your book.

The ultimate goal here is to have conversations. Driving traffic to your email list and then sending them a weekly email is not a relationship. I can tell you that I have never gotten a warm, fuzzy connection feeling from an email. However, I get that feeling all of the time from conversations.

Now It's Your Turn!

Go through your own funnels and determine where you can place your quiz for maximum effectiveness.

Traffic Temperature and Conversion

When we talk about traffic types, we also acknowledge that there is cold, warm, and hot traffic. This is why we break down the commitment section of our assessment marketing into high, medium, and low. What we are really looking at is hot, medium, or cold traffic. The traffic we own is generally medium or hot. Medium traffic needs to be nurtured and hot traffic is ready to close.

The way we speak to and what we provide to each of these traffic types varies. It is not a one-size-fits-all proposition. When we look at time and attention spent on these traffic modes, we need to be cognizant of our income-producing activities. Hot traffic are those people who come through our assessment as highly committed.

Cold traffic is traffic that we collect from ads or from the Internet. Many people who hire a digital marketing firm have expectations that the ads will create instant clicks and instant sales. This could not be further from the truth. The first digital marketing campaigns usually revolve around awareness. That means that consumers need to see your brand a minimum of seven times to begin to recognize your brand. That does not mean that the consumer knows, likes, or trusts you. It simply means that there is awareness you exist and maybe a little bit of curiosity about you. Any expectation that this traffic will convert is unrealistic.

Warm traffic occurs when someone has become more familiar with who you are and the value you provide. This is what nurture campaigns are all about. This phase is crucial to converting a prospect into a buyer. One of the huge mistakes that businesses make is going for the sale before the consumer is ready. This is where the process feels salesy because the marketing phase has failed to convert cold traffic to warm traffic before trying to sell.

Hot traffic is the best traffic because there is an established trust bond. This trust occurs because there is a relationship that has been built. This is especially crucial in the coaching world because so many consumers have been burned and are reluctant to purchase big- ticket items without a relationship. The relationship can be built through personal connection with the consumer or a referral from a trusted partner.

Knowing your traffic types and the temperature of your traffic can help you understand what level of language you use with a potential client. If you know your numbers, with regard to sales closing relationships, you can accurately begin to gauge your income in a more meaningful way. In other words, if I keep track of contacts in my CRM, I know that I it usually takes four calls to close a warm prospect. Keeping track of the number of calls and/ or contact from your income-producing activities and making sure that you schedule these activities daily will increase your revenue generation dramatically.

Now It's Your Turn!

1. Go through your own funnels and determine what kind of traffic you are attracting.

CHAPTER 10

ETHICAL ENROLLMENT

E thical enrollment is a reputation builder. There is nothing worse than being the small business that is known for shoving people into products just for the money. Your integrity is at stake and ensuring that people are in the right product for the level that meets their needs is essential. I was selling from a stage in Utah and after I pitched a $25,000 package. A gentleman approached me after my talk and wanted to purchase the program on the spot. After sitting down and finding out where he was today and where he wanted to be, I determined he was a candidate for my entry-level program. He said yes.

Now, I might sound like the worst salesperson on the planet but here's the deal. If you oversell and the client does not achieve the results you promised, it is always your fault. This person may not show up or work the program the way you would like but I can guarantee that he will tell the world that your product is crap because he didn't get results. When I stepped back and sold my new client the program that was at the level he needed today, I created a bond of trust. I wasn't going to take his money for the sake of more dollars in my bank account. I wanted to serve him in a way that would allow him to succeed. After he completed his starter program, he came back and bought the next-level program. This continued until he purchased his way into that big program he originally wanted. As a bonus, he has also been one of my greatest referral sources because I acted with integrity from the beginning.

Why Are Sales Conversations So Difficult?

There I was, on a call with the first person that was a candidate for our new $25,000 publishing package. I had my talking points, my deliverables, and everything I needed to have a conversation with this new prospect. Then it happened…I got to the price point and I stuttered. Literally stuttered, the words "twenty-five thousand" would not come out of my open mouth. I was shocked! At that moment, I realized that I was suffering from the same ailment that I teach my clients to overcome…the sales zone.

Let's face it, many of us have a lot riding on "yes." One of the old pillars of sales is convincing the prospect that he needs our product or service. We all know about the stereotype of the "fast-talking sales guy" whom we all hate. We don't like it when that guy sells to us and we do not want to be that guy when we sell. We avoid telemarketing calls because we hate that guy. Most of us will do anything to avoid being that guy and yet, we know we have to sell to make money. The struggle is real!

This is where the new sales rules come into play. Out with the old, high- pressure selling techniques that we have grown to abhor and in with the new sales techniques that create good feelings about selling.

The shift that occurs in today's selling world is from convincing to service- driven selling. There are five key points that are part of any service-driven conversation:

1. Service
2. Authenticity

3. Loyalty
4. Empowerment
5. Support

Service

When you approach sales with a mission to serve, you realize that every sales encounter is an opportunity to create transformation in someone else's life or business. Every sales conversation becomes a feel-good moment.

Authenticity

Products will come and go. The one constant in all of your business is YOU! People hire you or don't hire you because of how they resonate with you. Show up authentically and give people a reason to hire you. When you show up as your genuine self and your potential clients see that you care, it is easier for them to say "yes."

Loyalty

Be loyal to integrity and sell the right product to the right person. When you act from integrity in a sales situation and make it about the prospect and not the money, good things happen. Sell people the product that matches their skill level and be loyal to their success.

Empowerment

When you come to a sales conversation knowing where your prospect is today and where they would like to be six months from now, you open doors to possibility for them. Always explore the gap between where they are today and where they want to be six-months from now, so that they have the ability to paint an empowering portrait of what that looks like in their head.

Support

Being in support of your potential client's success is key to closing the deal. Communicating what your deliverables are in a way that nurtures their doubts and fears makes you an easy choice.

Now It's Your Turn!

Which one of the five SALES points is your strength and why?

Which one of the five SALES points do you need to improve and why?

Five Easy Steps to a Yes!

As you embrace more communication and relationship building with potential clients, there are key steps to make sure that you follow carefully. It is often helpful to look at these steps and practice them with each call until they become second nature. These are:

Build Trust and Relationships
Explore the Gap
Communicate Solutions
Invite with Integrity
Address Objections

1: Build Trust and Relationships

Most people who purchase from us either already know us or are referred from trusted sources.

Our main focus in this step is to welcome, communicate appreciation of their time, and make an emotional connection. If you do not have a personal connection previous to the call, this is the time to establish this connection.

The point of this step is to allow the prospect to feel seen, heard, and valued. Your main tool for this is the quiz results. Before the call, be sure you are familiar with their areas of strengths, areas of weakness, and also what level of experience you are speaking to.

You want to congratulate the prospect on their strengths and what they are doing well. Also, verify the level of expertise so you are speaking to them in the language that makes the most sense. (i.e. beginner, been in business for a while)

2: Explore the Gap

This is the listening phase. Let the prospect tell you what is not working for them and paint a vision of where they would like to be six months from now. Ask questions when necessary but do not sell. This is their time to reflect and communicate their wants and needs. Listen carefully. Their wants and needs will reveal themselves and can help you create an offer that meets them where they are at and leads them to where they want to be. All offers should be ethically aligned with wants and needs.

3: Communicate Solutions

This is where you transform the conversation into the shifts that are being sought. A good way to begin is to affirm what you were told and make sure that what you heard is what was communicated to you. Clarify their desires for shifts and improvements. When you are both in agreement about the desire of the potential client, ask permission to share a solution.

4: Invite with Integrity

Based on the prospect's desires, goals, and level of expertise, extend an offer that is in alignment with where this will lead. If possible, use a visual to help clarify the understanding of the deliverables of the program or service. After your explanation, ask about their level of interest (ask for a 1-10 scale), what works for them, and what does not. This can be a little scary, but it is such an important step because it allows you to keep improving based on real- life feedback.

5: Address Objections

This is what is known as "overcoming objections." We want to find out why the prospect has concerns about purchasing. Possibilities include doubts, fear, money, time, or even a disappointing experience from the past where the deliverables were not articulated clearly.

The Fortune is in the Follow Up

Not everyone is going to be an instant yes. When the call ends with a maybe or a no, ask when a good time would be to follow up. Then mark it in your calendar or CRM. This is an important step to continuing to build a relationship.

Every week, I have a spreadsheet built out from my calendar that is my follow-up for the week. If possible, make a phone call. Texting and email are not as personal and allows people to ignore you. Many of my prospects have been on my list for a year before they purchase. If you are someone who avoids this task, I encourage you to examine yourself as to why.

A good follow-up plan also includes how many contacts you are reaching weekly as well as the number of calls you make to one person for a yes. Many entrepreneurs have a difficult time forecasting their income. If you keep track of your closing rate, you will have a much easier time gauging your income. For example, if you know that you average two calls for every warm lead and five calls for cold leads, you can extrapolate how many calls you need to make a month to calculate your projected income.

For more about follow- up techniques, listen to our Promote, Profit, Publish interview with follow-up expert, Debbie Hoffman. https://superbrandpublishing.com/power-up-your-follow-up-with-debbie-hoffman/

CONCLUSION

For authors, coaches, and speakers, validation and conversations are crucial. The "bootstrap your way to bankruptcy" model of the coaching industry doesn't serve anyone.

My advice to entrepreneurs who are new to the marketplace is be realistic. The coaching industry is not an easy, slam-dunk money maker. You need a sustainable idea/ product that is validated with a validated audience. Make sure that this piece is completed before you jump in and purchase anything else.

Marketing depends on your audience knowing, liking, and trusting you. Don't buy into the digital hype and begin scaling a business before you have one that is consistently producing clients and making money. Have real conversations with real people and build relationships. Digital marketing is not only difficult, it can waste time and money chasing shiny objects.

Take one of our assessments and find out more about your skillset:

https://www.pitchslappedquiz.com.

Want to learn more about how to build your own lead generating assessments? Sign up for our Quiz Bootcamps: https://www.quizbootcamp.com/

Listen to our Promote, Profit, Publish podcast! Subscribe and get more tips to everyday marketing problems: https://podcasts.apple.com/us/podcast/promote-profit-publish/id1445478653

www.ingramcontent.com/pod-product-compliance
Lightning Source LLC
Chambersburg PA
CBHW070833180526
45168CB00002B/822